Developing
Grade 3 Reading Fluency

Written by
Trisha Callella

Editor: Teri L. Applebaum
Illustrator: Jane Yamada
Cover Illustrator: Chris Ellithorpe
Designer: Mary Gagné
Cover Designer: Mary Gagné
Art Director: Tom Cochrane
Project Director: Carolea Williams

Table of Contents

Introduction

Learning to read is a systematic, learned process. Once students can read individual words, they need to learn to put those words together to form sentences. Then, students must learn to read those sentences fluently to comprehend not only the meaning of each word but also the meaning of an entire sentence. Students' reading fluency develops as they learn to break sentences into phrases and to "chunk" words together into phrases as they read. As students read sentences in phrases, they develop better comprehension of each sentence's meaning.

Use the lessons in *Developing Reading Fluency* to meet district, state, and national reading standards as you teach students how to develop reading fluency. The first four sections are arranged sequentially to help you implement fluency modeling, fluency practice by students, and then students' application of fluency strategies. Use the activities to help students build upon the skills they learned in the previous section. The final two sections of the book contain additional instruction to provide intervention for students having difficulties. The book features the following strategies to improve students' reading fluency:

- **Interactive Read-Alouds:** Use modeled and choral reading with the whole class or small groups to increase students' listening comprehension and to give them experience with rereading short rhymed phrases.
- **Read-Arounds:** Help students learn high-frequency and content words and practice reading text in phrases as they work in small groups.
- **Plays for Two:** Use these simple scripts to have students practice with a partner repeated oral reading strategies as they develop phrasing and fluency.
- **Reader's Theater:** Have students work in groups of four to practice rereading a script until they can fluently read their part in front of an audience. Use the performances as a culminating activity to have students apply all the reading strategies they have learned.
- **Phrasing Memory Challenges:** Invite students who are still not reading with phrasing and fluency to use their auditory memory to repeat phrases as you or a peer tutor models correct reading.
- **Intervention Instruction:** Use these activities with individuals or small groups to intervene with students who still struggle with reading fluency. These activities enable students to identify and practice expression, intonation, and the natural flow of fluency.

The activities in this book provide students with a variety of reading experiences. The themes and genres included in each section will motivate students to not only read the text but to read with expression, intonation, and a natural flow. Students will build enthusiasm and confidence as they begin to increase their comprehension and as they successfully apply reading strategies to their everyday reading!

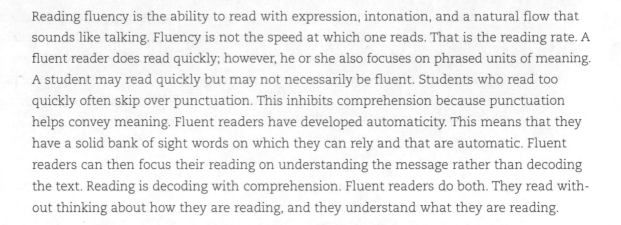

Fluency

Reading fluency is the ability to read with expression, intonation, and a natural flow that sounds like talking. Fluency is not the speed at which one reads. That is the reading rate. A fluent reader does read quickly; however, he or she also focuses on phrased units of meaning. A student may read quickly but may not necessarily be fluent. Students who read too quickly often skip over punctuation. This inhibits comprehension because punctuation helps convey meaning. Fluent readers have developed automaticity. This means that they have a solid bank of sight words on which they can rely and that are automatic. Fluent readers can then focus their reading on understanding the message rather than decoding the text. Reading is decoding with comprehension. Fluent readers do both. They read without thinking about how they are reading, and they understand what they are reading.

What does a child who lacks fluency sound like?

A student who lacks fluency may sound choppy, robotic, or speedy.

How does repeated oral reading increase fluency?

Research shows that students increase their fluency when they read and reread the same passage aloud several times. The support that teachers give students during oral reading by modeling the text and providing guidance and feedback enhances their fluency development. Using this strategy, students gradually become better readers and their word recognition, speed, accuracy, and fluency all increase as a result. Their comprehension also improves because they are bridging the gap between reading for word recognition and reading for meaning.

Should I worry about fluency with students who are emergent readers?

Bad habits can be hard to break. Research has found that poor reading habits stand in the way of students becoming fluent readers. Research has also found that students can and do become fluent even as emergent readers. Those emergent, fluent readers carry that fluency onto more difficult text and therefore have a higher level of comprehension. Fluency activities should be incorporated into every classroom, beginning in kindergarten with modeled reading, shared reading, guided reading, and independent reading.

How do fluency and phrasing work together?

Phrasing is the link between decoding the meaning of the text and reading the text fluently. Phrasing is the way that a reader groups the words. A lack of phrasing results in staccato reading, "word calling," and decoding. A fluent reader reads quickly in phrased chunks that are meaningful. Read the information on page 5 to learn more about phrasing.

Phrasing

A student who reads in phrases reads words in meaningful groups. Phrasing helps a student understand that the text carries meaning. A phrase is a group of words that the reader says together and reads together. The way the words are grouped affects the meaning. This is why phrasing affects reading comprehension.

What does phrasing sound like?

Consider how the same sentence can have different meanings depending on the way the words are grouped, or phrased. It clearly affects the comprehension of what is read. For example:

Patti Lee is my best friend.

Patti, Lee is my best friend.

Who is the best friend? It depends on how the sentence is read. In this example, punctuation also affects phrasing.

What causes incorrect phrasing?

A student may read with incorrect phrasing for a number of reasons. First of all, many students rely too much on phonics. This leads to a dependency on decoding. When students focus on decoding, they neglect the message. They turn into expert "word callers." Incorrect phrasing can also result from a lack of attention to punctuation. Some students ignore punctuation altogether, which will result in incorrect phrasing, will affect their fluency, and will hurt their comprehension.

What can I do to teach and improve phrasing?

1. Use the activities in this book. They are all researched, teacher-tested, and student-approved, and they will help students experience reading fluency success.

2. Stop pointing to each word during shared reading because that reinforces word-by-word reading. Once students can point and read with one-to-one correspondence, begin shared reading with a finger sweep under phrases. (Finger sweeps look like a stretched out "u.") This strategy models and reinforces phrasing.

3. Read and reread.

4. Model. Model. Model.

5. Echo read.

6. Make flash cards of common phrases to help students train their eyes to see words in groups rather than as individual words.

7. Tape-record students as they read. Let them listen to improvements they make in phrasing and intonation.

How to Use This Book

The activities in this book provide fun and easy strategies that will help students develop reading fluency. Getting started is simple.

- Use the Stages of Fluency Development chart on page 7 to assess the students' ability. Take notes as students read aloud, and then refer to the chart to see at what stage of fluency development they are. Use this information to create a plan of action and to decide on which skills the whole class, groups of students, and individuals need to focus.
- Use the Fantastic Five Format on page 8 with the whole class, small groups, or individuals. This format provides a guideline for developing reading fluency that will work with any genre. Copy the reproducible, and use it as a "cheat sheet" when you give guided instruction. You will find the format effective in helping you with modeling, teaching, guiding, and transferring phrased and fluent reading to independent reading.
- Refer to the Teacher Tips on page 9 before you begin using the activities in this book. These tips include helpful information that will assist you as you teach all the students in your classroom to read fluently and, as a result, improve their comprehension of text.

Fluency Activities and Strategies

The first four sections of this book have been sequentially arranged for you to first model fluency, then have students practice fluency, and finally have them independently apply their newly learned skills. Each section has an introductory page to help you get started. It includes

- an explanation of how the activities in that section relate to fluency development
- the strategies students will use to complete the activities
- a materials list
- step-by-step directions for preparing and presenting the activities
- an idea for how to extend the activities

Each section opener is followed by a set of fun reproducible reading materials that are designed to excite and motivate students about developing reading fluency. Within each section, the readability of the reproducibles increases in difficulty to provide appropriate reading material for third graders who read at different levels.

Intervention Activities and Strategies

The last two sections of the book provide additional instruction and practice to help students who have difficulty with reading fluency. The Phrasing Memory Challenges section contains several readings designed to be used one-on-one between a teacher or peer and a struggling student. The Intervention Instruction section contains several activities designed for use with individuals or small groups. Each activity has its own page of directions that lists strategies, an objective, materials, and step-by-step directions. Reassess students often to determine their reading fluency level and their need for intervention.

Stages of Fluency Development

Stage	What You Observe	What to Teach for Fluency
1	• many miscues • too much emphasis on meaning • storytelling based on pictures • sounds fluent but not reading what is written down • playing "teacher" while reading	• print carries the meaning
2	• tries to match what he or she says with what is written on the page • one-to-one correspondence • finger pointing and "voice pointing" • staccato reading, robotic reading	• phrasing and fluency • focus on meaning • read like talking • high-frequency words • purpose of punctuation
3	• focuses on the meaning of print • may use bookmarks • focuses more on print than picture • no longer voice points • laughs, giggles, or comments while reading	• phrasing and fluency • focus on what makes sense and looks right • purpose of punctuation • proper expression and intonation
4	• reads books with more print than pictures • wants to talk about what he or she read • reads like talking with phrasing • reads punctuation with expression • laughs, giggles, or comments while reading	• shades of meaning • making connections

Fantastic Five Format

Step 1

Modeled Fluency

Model reading with fluency so that students understand the text and what they are supposed to learn.

Step 2

Echo Reading

Read one part. Have students repeat the same part.

Step 3

Choral Reading

Read together. This prepares students to take over the task of reading.

Step 4

Independent Fluency

Have students read to you.

Step 5

Reverse Echo Reading

Have students read to you, and then repeat their phrasing, expression, and fluency. Students have now taken over the task of reading.

Developing Reading Fluency • Gr. 3 © 2003 Creative Teaching Press

1. Be aware of how you arrange rhymes, stories, and poems in a pocket chart. Often, teachers put each line in a separate pocket. When teachers do this, students do not recognize phrases and they begin to think that sentences always end on the right. (That is one reason why students often put a period at the end of every line in their writing journals.) Instead, cut the sentences or rhymes into meaningful phrased chunks so that students see and read what you model and teach.

2. If you use guided reading in your classroom, incorporate time for children to reread familiar books. Keep guided reading books that were once used for instructional purposes in bins that are color-coded to represent different ability levels. Have each student choose a book to reread as a warm-up every time you meet. This helps students put phrasing and fluency instruction into practice. Remember, use books that are appropriate to students' independent-reading level (books that can be read with 95 percent accuracy).

3. Write a daily Morning Message that follows a predictable format. Follow the Fantastic Five Format on page 8 to develop phrasing and fluency and improve reading comprehension.

4. Have a Student of the Day tell you three things about himself or herself. Model for the class how to write the student's information in phrases on a piece of white construction paper. Read it in phrases and choral read it for fluency. Reread all of the information about previous Students of the Day prior to writing about the new Student. Bind the pages together into a class book, and have students read it independently or take it home to share with their family.

5. Once a student matches speech to print, do not allow him or her to point when reading. It is important to train students' eyes to look at words in groups rather than at one word at a time. While reading aloud, fluent readers look at many words ahead of what they read.

6. If students must use bookmarks to track words as they read, have them hold the bookmark just above the line of print they are reading rather than just under the line. When students use a bookmark under a line of print, the bookmark blocks the next line. This keeps students from reading fluently because they cannot see the ending punctuation. Try it—you will find that you cannot read fluently with a bookmark under the line you read. You will be amazed how this small change affects students' reading.

Learn to read with fluency !

Getting Started

Interactive Read-Alouds

Comprehension begins at the listening stage. Students understand what they hear before they understand what they read. That is why research supports reading aloud to students books and stories that are above their reading level. Reading aloud builds vocabulary, models thinking aloud, and models phrasing and fluency. This activity takes reading aloud a step further by including rhymed phrases that students will then use to apply the repeated oral reading strategy. The structure of this activity will keep students actively listening.

Strategies: repeated oral reading, modeled fluency, choral reading, active listening

Materials
• overhead projector/transparencies or chart paper (optional)

Directions

1. Choose one story, and make one copy of the reproducible. (The stories "The Magic Coin" and "Kindness Counts!" have two pages.) Copy a class set of the corresponding rhymed phrases. Or, as an option, make an overhead transparency of the reproducible or write the rhymed phrases on the board or chart paper.

2. NOTE: Do not photocopy the story for students. This activity is designed to build students' listening comprehension. They need to hear phrasing and fluency modeled by you in order to replicate it in their own reading.

3. Give each student a copy of the rhymed phrases, or display the phrases so all the students can see them. Read aloud the phrases, and have students practice reading them. Tell students that you will read aloud a story and that they will read aloud the rhymed phrases each time you point to them. (Point to the class each time you see an asterisk in the story.)

4. Read aloud the story. Model good phrasing, intonation, and fluency.

5. Throughout the story, stop at each asterisk, point to the students, and have them read the rhymed phrases, with increased fluency each time.

Extension

Many of the rhymed phrases lend themselves to movements. Make up silly movements that students can do as they read their part. This will maximize active listening. Try movements such as clicking tongues, clapping, stomping feet, moving hands like waves in the ocean, moving hands up together and then parting them in opposite ways, nodding heads, hopping, turning around, and cross-lateral movements.

The Magic Coin

I know you will have a hard time believing what I'm about to tell you, but I promise it's the whole truth and nothing but the truth. It all started the night after my birthday party. I was helping my mom clean up and putting my toys away like any other ordinary day. Suddenly, I discovered that there was something rattling in the bottom of one of my gift boxes. I was sure that I had taken all of the gifts out of the boxes as I opened them. How could I have left a gift behind? Nobody forgets or loses birthday presents! I shook the box again. Sure enough, there was definitely something still in that box. I lifted up the tissue paper and found a large, shiny gold coin. It looked very old. I had never seen such a coin before. I bit into it thinking it might be chocolate. No such luck! It was just a strange, shiny gold coin that was probably not worth anything at all. I put it in my pocket as I continued cleaning. As I was throwing away the last of the wrapping paper, I came up with a little rhyme for my coin. It went like this: ✳

Suddenly, the coin started to move around in my pocket! I jumped so high that I dropped all of the wrapping paper. It kept moving around. What in the world was happening? I took it out of my pocket and looked at it. It looked the same, but it felt a bit warm in my hand. I didn't know what to do. It reminded me of a story I once read. The boy in the story got to make a wish. I thought to myself, *What harm could it be? Nobody will know I made a silly wish.* Then, I said my rhyme again: ✳

The coin started jumping around in my hand! It was a bit scary I must admit. I made one tiny wish and flipped the coin. ✳ All of a sudden, the coin was perfectly still in my hand. It didn't move one bit. Did my wish make it stop? No way! Impossible! That was just something writers made up in books. My imagination was really getting out of control. Maybe it was all that birthday cake and ice cream.

Interactive Read-Alouds

The Magic Coin

I finished cleaning up and joined my dad in the kitchen. He was busy making my favorite meal of spaghetti with peanut butter sauce. It was my annual birthday meal. After dinner, I went up to my room to get ready for bed. All of a sudden, something popped into my head. You guessed it. ✻ The coin started moving around in my pocket again. Oh, no! Now what? I made another wish and it stopped right away. Was this really a magic coin? Did my wish come true? Impossible! I had better try it again. I must be dreaming. Once again, the coin started moving around! I made a wish, flipped the coin again, and then it suddenly stopped moving. This coin was beginning to scare me. I decided to put the coin in a safe place for the night. I told myself not to say, ✻

I figured that the safest place for the coin would be inside of a sock in my drawer. Then, if it moved, it wouldn't wake me up. I closed the drawer tightly. Safe! Nobody would ever know it existed. I figured I could just forget about it, so that's just what I did. Every time I thought of the rhyme, ✻ I told myself to forget about it.

The next morning, I woke up like usual and crawled out of bed. I love school, but sometimes it's hard to get up so early in the morning. Suddenly, I tripped and fell. What made me fall? I turned on the light above my bed and looked around.

OH, NO! All around me there were toys! There were games, puzzles, cars, construction sets, books, stuffed animals, electronic games, every toy you could imagine. It looked like a toy store. OH, NO! What happened? Was this my room? It looked like my room—same wallpaper, same bed, same lights. Was it the same floor? I couldn't tell, since the floor was covered in toys. THE COIN! It was magic! My first wish had come true. I wished that I could have a whole room of toys for my birthday. It came true. What would my parents do? I had to get rid of the toys before my family saw how greedy I was. Why did I ever touch that coin? Why did I ever make up that rhyme? ✻ Why was I so greedy? I had to get that coin and make a new wish that everything would go away.

I hopped over and around all of the toys until I reached my sock drawer. Thank goodness, the coin was still there. I had to make new wishes to make sure the others didn't come true. They were silly wishes as well. I didn't really want cake for every meal. I didn't really wish that I had a red sports car—well, maybe—but I couldn't drive it. I had to hurry up and say the rhyme: ✻ Will it work?

Developing Reading Fluency • Gr. 3 © 2003 Creative Teaching Press

The Magic Coin
Rhymed Phrases

Magic coin! Magic coin! I'll rub you in my hand.

Magic coin! Magic coin! I'll toss you in the air.

Magic coin! Magic coin! I don't know how you'll land.

Magic coin! Magic coin! Heads or tails? I don't care!

- -

The Magic Coin
Rhymed Phrases

Magic coin! Magic coin! I'll rub you in my hand.

Magic coin! Magic coin! I'll toss you in the air.

Magic coin! Magic coin! I don't know how you'll land.

Magic coin! Magic coin! Heads or tails? I don't care!

Developing Reading Fluency • Gr. 3 © 2003 Creative Teaching Press

The Flu

Hello, boys and girls! I'm your school nurse. I came here today to talk to you about ways to stay healthy. I have just returned from a conference held by the United States Centers for Disease Control and Prevention. I learned some helpful tips, which I am here to share with you. First of all, let's warm up with a little healthy reminder: *

Good! Now that we all know that we'd rather be healthy than stuck inside, sick in bed, let's learn a few facts about the flu. The flu (technically called influenza) is a highly contagious infection of the nose, throat, and lungs. It is one of the worst illnesses of the winter season. It is caused by a virus and is spread easily from person to person through sneezing and coughing. Some symptoms include high fever, chills, dry cough, headache, runny nose, sore throat, an upset stomach, and muscle pain. It makes you very tired. Sound like fun? No way! What do we say? *

You might be surprised to hear that approximately one to two out of every ten people will get the flu this year! Yes, that means that the chances of some of you being sick in bed for days or even weeks are high. Your chances are high because kids share the same room, touch the same items, and often forget to wash their hands as often as they should. What do we say? Flu, no way! *

If you really want to do your best to avoid getting stuck in bed and feeling miserable from the flu virus, there are some things you can do. Prevention is the key. Some of you may have already gotten a flu shot. If you did, then you probably don't have to worry about catching the flu virus this year. However, you will need to get a new shot next year. If you did not get a shot and do not plan on getting one, then you really need to go out of your way to make sure you wash your hands, sneeze and cough into your arm, and stay away from people who sneeze and cough. What do we say? Flu, go away! *

What if you get the flu? Well, you will need to visit the doctor to see if you need medicine. Then, you will have to get plenty of rest and drink lots of fluids. The goal should always be prevention. If you are aware of healthy, hygienic behaviors, you should be able to avoid the flu this year. Is the flu going to get you? No way! Flu, go away! We don't want the flu this year, so we say, *

Developing Reading Fluency • Gr. 3 © 2003 Creative Teaching Press

The Flu
Rhymed Phrases

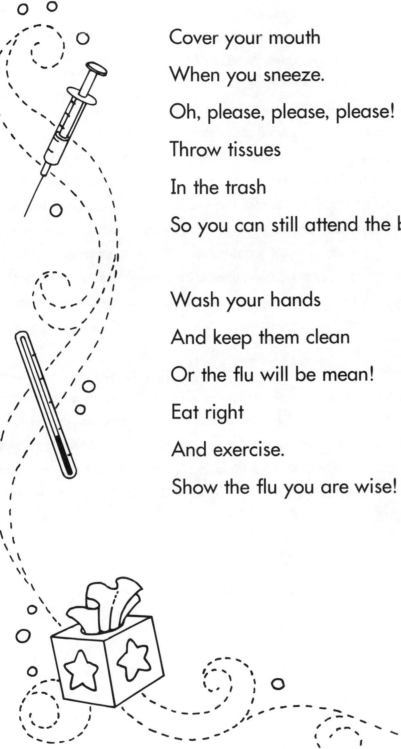

Cover your mouth

When you sneeze.

Oh, please, please, please!

Throw tissues

In the trash

So you can still attend the bash!

Wash your hands

And keep them clean

Or the flu will be mean!

Eat right

And exercise.

Show the flu you are wise!

Theme: *character education*

Be Kind!

Frankie Phillips called the meeting to order. "Okay, Kids of Kindness. Our third official meeting is now called to order. What is our motto?" ✻ "That's right! That's why we're here. That's why we say our Kids of Kindness Cheer. Go Kids! Go Kids! Go, go, go! We have tons of kindness that we will show!"

"Now, let's get down to business. At our last meeting, we found out about some families who didn't have any money for winter clothes for their growing children. What should we do?" ✻

"Well, that all sounds terrific, but we can't do it all. What should we do to help the families and children who need clothes?" Taylor raised his hand and said, "I went home and told my grandma about the problem. She had a great idea. She said that we should hold a clothing drive. We could tell all of our friends and family to go through their closets and look for any clothes they don't want or need anymore. We could collect the clothes and then donate them."

"What do the rest of the Kids of Kindness think of Taylor's idea?" asked Frankie. ✻ "Terrific! It's settled. We're planning a clothing drive. Let's focus on the details. Who will make the flyers so that everyone knows why we are doing it? Who will collect the clothes and who will pick up the clothes?"

Within a half hour, the clothing drive was planned and organized. Mick's grandpa would collect the clothes and deliver them, since he drove a big van. Melissa's mom would make the flyers. Claudia, Zack, and Carlos would photocopy the flyers when they were ready. Kevin would make an announcement to the student council to see if they wanted to help out. Everyone else would go through their closets and tell all of their friends. Before they all left, they said their Kids of Kindness motto one more time. ✻

Developing Reading Fluency • Gr. 3 © 2003 Creative Teaching Press

Kindness Counts!

Be Kind!

At their next meeting, two weeks later, Frankie announced, "I am happy to call this meeting to order and to tell you that we have been successful! After only three meetings, we have already put our motto into practice! Let's all give a good Kids of Kindness cheer." ✱ "Yes, we have enough clothes for every single family on our list. No child will be left without clothes this winter. Congratulations! We can now move on to the agenda for today. Who has an idea that we can work on to spread our kindness even further?"

A new child in the back raised her hand. "I just heard about your club. My name is Trisha. I would like to join if we can include acts of kindness toward animals in the club's goals. I think we should collect cans of dog and cat food, old blankets, and dog bones to donate to the local animal shelters. I just adopted an old cat from the animal shelter, and I overheard some of the people saying that their funds are short this year. They were worried about having enough money to care for the animals until they are adopted. Would the Kids of Kindness be willing to do that?"

"What do we all think of Trisha's idea?" asked Frankie. ✱ "Well, Trisha, that's our way of saying yes. By the way, we would love to have you as a member of our club. We like the way you think of all living things—human and animal alike. We've helped the people in need; now it's time to help the animals in need. All those in favor of helping the animal shelters yell *Kids of Kindness*. That clearly passed. Let's get on with the details. First, we'll need a list of ideas for the flyer. Trisha, you came up with some good ones. I think we may be able to add a few more to the list. Does the animal shelter care for birds as well? Perhaps we should include birdseed on our list."

This time, the club only took 15 minutes to organize a plan. Everyone was so excited to have a new service project. They were thrilled to have another opportunity to make a difference. They couldn't wait to help out again. ✱ Do you think that they met their goals? Would you have helped out with either project? Can you think of any other ways people can help others?✱

Developing Reading Fluency • Gr. 3 © 2003 Creative Teaching Press

Interactive Read-Alouds

Kindness Counts!
Rhymed Phrases

Volunteer! Donate!

Do something to make someone else feel great!

Share a dollar or even just a dime.

Give somebody a little more of your time.

Get rid of your greed.

Help someone else who is in need.

It doesn't matter the amount.

Every bit of kindness will always count!

Developing Reading Fluency • Gr. 3 © 2003 Creative Teaching Press

Food Chain Rap

(Teacher: Read the first paragraph as a rap.)

Let's review what we know about food chains. Yes, you know they are a little like trains. There's the engine that pulls the rest of the cars. In the food chain, it's the sun, not the stars.

Okay, that's enough of my rhyming and rapping parts. The rest will be up to you. As we learn a bit more about food chains, you'll be helping me out with our Food Chain Rap.

A food chain explains how living things eat other living things in order to survive. We all need to understand how important the sun is to all food chains. ✳ The producers are in the first train car behind the engine. A plant is a producer because it can make food from nonliving things. The consumers are in the next three train cars. A consumer is a living thing that eats something for its food. Do you know all about consumers? The consumers are the herbivores, carnivores, and omnivores. Herbivores are plant eaters. They eat the producers. Carnivores are meat eaters. They eat other animals. Omnivores eat meat and plants. ✳

The last link in the food chain is very important. At the end of the train are the decomposers. They are like nature's garbage disposals. These fungi and bacteria help dead plants and animals to decay. Some animal scavengers help the decomposers by eating the remains of dead plants and animals. The decomposers help keep the earth clean and healthy. Without them, the world would be quite stinky! ✳

There are food chains in every habitat. There are food chains in the ocean, the desert, the grassland, and the forests. In every food chain of every environment, the food chain train is driven by the energy of the sun. There is always some type of green plant as a producer. The plants get eaten by consumers. Finally, the decay of dead plants and animals provide food for the decomposers. Then, the cycle starts all over again. Some people call it the circle of life since it has no end. It repeats itself over and over again. ✳

Let's look at a food chain in action. First, we have the sun, which helps the plant leaves make food. The leaves may be eaten by a caterpillar. The caterpillar is eaten by a spider. The spider is eaten by a bird. When this bird unfortunately dies, it will decompose and provide nourishment for the decomposers, such as insects, worms, and mushrooms. 'Round and 'round the food chain goes. If it ever stops, then nothing will grow! ✳

Interactive Read-Alouds

Food Chain Rap
Rhymed Phrases

The food chain begins with the sunlight.

It gives energy for living things to grow.

Producers, consumers, decomposers—that's right!

They are the links in the food chain you know.

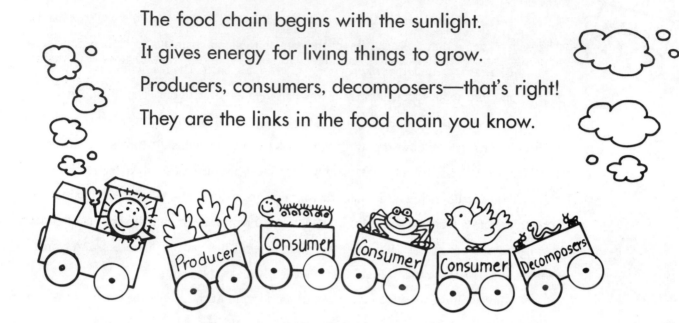

Food Chain Rap
Rhymed Phrases

The food chain begins with the sunlight.

It gives energy for living things to grow.

Producers, consumers, decomposers—that's right!

They are the links in the food chain you know.

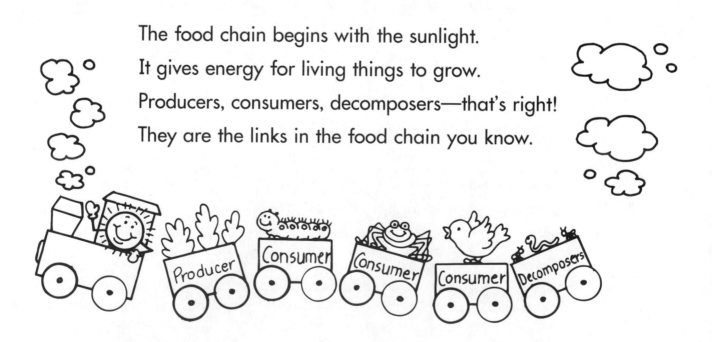

Developing Reading Fluency • Gr. 3 © 2003 Creative Teaching Press

According to research, one reason why students do not read with phrasing and fluency is that they do not have a solid base of high-frequency words and sight words, which is required for reading books independently. Research recommends activities that give students practice with frequently used words. This will in turn help with phrasing and fluency because students will not need to slow down to decode as often. The Read-Around cards in this section are already written in phrases (spaces between groups of words), so students can see and better understand how to read words in groups. The Read-Around cards are designed for groups of two to four students. This allows for optimal amounts of practice and active involvement. The phrases on the cards are short and simple to help students focus directly on reading phrases and practicing high-frequency and content words.

Strategies: phrased reading; repeated oral reading; active listening; reading high-frequency, content, and sight words

Materials
- construction paper or tagboard
- scissors
- envelopes

Directions

1. Choose a set of cards (e.g., synonyms, measurement), and copy the cards on construction paper or tagboard. (Each set of cards is two pages.) Cut apart the cards, and laminate them so that they can be reused throughout the school year. Put the cards in an envelope, and write the title (e.g., *Synonyms*) on the envelope.

2. Give a set of cards to a small group of students so that each student has one to three cards. Review with students the pronunciation and meaning of the bold words and phrases on their clue cards so that they are familiar and comfortable with them (or preteach the words).

3. Explain that students will play a listening and reading game. Model how the game works and the correct answers with each group the first time students play using a new set of cards. Read aloud each student's cards, and then have students silently read their cards at least five times to build fluency. Discuss each question and corresponding answer so students can concentrate more on reading fluently than on determining the answer to the question as they play.

4. Tell the group that the student who has the clue card that says *I have the first card* will begin the game by reading aloud his or her card. After the first card is read aloud, have the student with the answer to the clue read aloud his or her card. Tell students to continue until they get back to the first card. (The game ends after a student reads *Who has the first card?* and a student answers *I have the first card.*)

5. Encourage students to play the game at least twice. Have them mix up the cards and pass the cards out again so that students read different cards each time.

Extension

Invite students to take home a set of cards. Have them teach their family how to play and practice reading the cards with family members. Encourage families to make additional cards.

Synonyms

I have   the first card.

Who has the word that means   the same as **idea**?

I have   the word **thought**.

Who has the word that means   the same as **praise**?

I have   the word **compliment.**

Who has the word that means   the same as **shy**?

I have   the word **timid**.

Who has the word that means   the same as **genuine**?

I have   the word **authentic**.

Who has the word that means   the same as **achieve**?

I have   the word **accomplish**.

Who has the word that means   the same as **clever**?

Developing Reading Fluency • Gr. 3 © 2003 Creative Teaching Press

Synonyms

I have   the word **brilliant**.

Who has the word that means   the same as **alert**?

I have   the word **attentive**.

Who has the word that means   the same as **careful**?

I have   the word **cautious**.

Who has the word that means   the same as **foolish**?

I have   the word **ridiculous**.

Who has the word that means   the same as **easy**?

I have   the word **uncomplicated**.

Who has the word that means   the same as **false**?

I have   the word **incorrect**.

Who has   the first card?

Read-Arounds

Antonyms

I have   the first card.

Who has the word that means   the opposite of **refuse**?

I have   the word **accept**.

Who has the word that means   the opposite of **introduction**?

I have   the word **conclusion**.

Who has the word that means   the opposite of **rude**?

I have   the word **courteous**.

Who has the word that means   the opposite of **increase**?

I have   the word **decrease**.

Who has the word that means   the opposite of **deny**?

I have   the word **accept**.

Who has the word that means   the opposite of **create**?

Antonyms

I have   the word **destroy**.

Who has the word that means   the opposite of **selfish**?

I have   the word **generous**.

Who has the word that means   the opposite of **perfect**?

I have   the word **imperfect.**

Who has the word that means   the opposite of **fake**?

I have   the word **authentic**.

Who has the word that means   the opposite of **loyal**?

I have   the word **disloyal**.

Who has the word that means   the opposite of **famous**?

I have   the word **unknown**.

Who has   the first card?

Developing Reading Fluency • Gr. 3 © 2003 Creative Teaching Press

Prefixes and Suffixes

I have   the first card.

Who has the name   of the **meaningful chunk**

that goes at the front of a word   **to change the meaning**?

I have   the word **prefix**.

Who has the name   of the **meaningful chunk**

that goes at the end of a word   **to change the meaning**?

I have   the word **suffix**.

Who has the **prefix**   that means **again**?

I have   the **prefix re-**.

Who has the **prefix**   that means **not**?

I have   the prefix **un-**.

Who has the **prefix**   that means **badly or wrongly**?

I have   the prefix **mis-**.

Who has the **prefix**   that means **two**?

Developing Reading Fluency • Gr. 3 © 2003 Creative Teaching Press

Prefixes and Suffixes

I have   the **prefix bi-**.

Who has the **prefix**   that means **before**?

I have   the **prefix pre-**.

Who has the **prefix**   that means **against**?

I have   the **prefix anti-**.

Who has the **prefix**   that means **after**?

I have   the **prefix post-**.

Who has the **suffix**   that means **full of**?

I have   the **suffix -ful**.

Who has the **suffix**   that means **most**?

I have   the **suffix -est**.

Who has the **suffix**   that means **more**?

I have   the **suffix -er**.

Who has   the first card?

Read-Arounds

Informational Materials

I have   the first card.

Who has the **place**   **you would look**   **for a word**
that means the same   **as another word?**

I have   the **thesaurus.**

Who has the **place**   **you would look**   **in a book**
to find out   **the names of the chapters?**

I have   the **table of contents.**

Who has the **place**   **you would look**   **for a definition**
of a word   **you don't know?**

I have   the **dictionary or glossary.**

Who has the **place**   **you would look**   **to find out**
where your city   **is located?**

I have   the **atlas.**

Who has the **place**   **you would look**   **in a book**
to find out   **which page talks about a certain topic?**

Developing Reading Fluency • Gr. 3 © 2003 Creative Teaching Press

Informational Materials

I have the **index**.

Who has the **place** you would look to learn about the first president of the United States?

I have the **encyclopedia or Internet**.

Who has the **place** you would look to find out the weather in your area today?

I have the **local newspaper or TV news broadcast**.

Who has the **definition** of the "www" that you type in when you go on the Internet?

I have the **World Wide Web**.

Who has the **word** that describes sending a letter electronically over the Internet?

I have the word **e-mail**.

Who has the **place** you can go to borrow a book that you want to read?

I have the **library**.

Who has the first card?

Developing Reading Fluency • Gr. 3 © 2003 Creative Teaching Press

Measurement

I have   the first card.

Who has the number   of **minutes in an hour**?

I have   the number **sixty**.

Who has the number   of **ounces in a pound**?

I have   the number **sixteen**.

Who has the number   of **dimes in a dollar**?

I have   the number **ten**.

Who has the number   of **quarts in a gallon**?

I have   the number **four**.

Who has the number   of **inches in a foot**?

I have   the number **twelve**.

Who has the number   of **feet in a yard**?

Developing Reading Fluency • Gr. 3 © 2003 Creative Teaching Press

Measurement

I have   the number **three**.

Who has the number   of **eggs in three dozen**?

I have   the number **thirty-six**.

Who has the number   of **hours in a day**?

I have   the number **twenty-four**.

Who has the number   of **days in two weeks**?

I have   the number **fourteen**.

Who has the number   of **weeks in a year**?

I have   the number **fifty-two**.

Who has the number   of **cups in a pint**?

I have   the number **two**.

Who has   the first card?

Read-Arounds

Multiplication Facts

I have the first card.

Who has the product of **five times seven**?

I have the number **thirty-five**.

Who has the product of **six times four**?

I have the number **twenty-four**.

Who has the product of **three times six**?

I have the number **eighteen**.

Who has the product of **nine times three**?

I have the number **twenty-seven**.

Who has the product of **five times five**?

I have the number **twenty-five**.

Who has the product of **zero times eight**?

Developing Reading Fluency • Gr. 3 © 2003 Creative Teaching Press

Multiplication Facts

I have   the number **zero**.

Who has the product   of **four times four**?

I have   the number **sixteen**.

Who has the product   of **six times two**?

I have   the number **twelve**.

Who has the product   of **three times seven**?

I have   the number **twenty-one**.

Who has the product   of **six times five**?

I have   the number **thirty**.

Who has the product   of **six times seven**?

I have   the number **forty-two**.

Who has   the first card?

Developing Reading Fluency • Gr. 3 © 2003 Creative Teaching Press

Read-Arounds

Plays for Two

Reading is a social event. People who enjoy books like to talk about them and recommend their favorite books. In classrooms, students are often asked to read alone. However, reading with a partner helps students develop phrasing and fluency through repeated oral reading while incorporating the social aspect of reading. Each Plays for Two story is designed for a pair of students to read together. Students will read their parts many times (repeated oral reading strategy) to improve their phrasing and fluency. Then, they will give a final reading for another pair, you, or the whole class. This activity helps reading take on a purpose.

Strategies: repeated oral reading, paired reading

Materials
- notebook/clear notebook sheet protectors

Directions

1. Make two single-sided copies of a paired reading script for each pair of students. (Each script is two pages long.) Do not copy the pages back-to-back. The print bleeds through and is visually distracting to students.
2. Divide the class into pairs. Give each pair a set of scripts.
3. Introduce the text to each pair through guided reading. Then, give partners time to practice reading together. (Have students practice reading and rereading many times to help them develop phrasing and fluency.)
4. To help students develop oral language and public speaking skills in front of a group, invite partners to "perform" their reading in front of the class or for a small group.
5. Train students to give each other specific compliments on their performance. Have them use the words and phrases *sounds like talking, phrasing,* and *fluent.*
6. Store each paired reading script in a clear notebook sheet protector (front to back). Store the sheet protectors in a notebook to make them easily accessible for future use.

Extension

Invite students to make cutouts of the characters and objects in the story to make it more interactive. Have students color the cutouts and glue them to craft sticks to use as props.

The Flood

Genre: narrative story

Characters: Reader 1 and Reader 2

Reader 1   Hurry up! Get your things out of the basement! The storm is getting worse!

Reader 2   I'm doing the best I can. The weather forecaster didn't say anything about the storm getting this powerful!

Reader 1   The homes around the block are already flooded. There's a chance that our home could become flooded, too!

Reader 2   This is the last box from the basement. Do we have enough sandbags around the outside of the house?

Reader 1   I sure hope so. It's too late to make any more right now.

Reader 2   Oh, no! Now our electricity has gone out. It's a good thing it's still daylight outside.

Reader 1   I'm going to pack up the cats. Will you please bring down the suitcases? We need to get out of here right away!

Reader 2   Sure. No problem. I'll put the suitcases and the cat food in the car. I'll meet you at the front door.

The Flood

Reader 1   Hurry! We don't have much time. We need to get on the road before it's too flooded. We've got to get to Grandpa's house. It'll be safer there.

Reader 2   Let's go!
(a few minutes later)

Reader 1   I've got the suitcases in the car.

Reader 2   I found the cats. I just can't catch Shadow. He's hiding under the bed in the corner where I can't reach him.

Reader 1   He's such a scaredy cat! I'll crawl under there and get him. I'm coming right now.

Reader 2   Thanks. Let's go!

Reader 1   I'll hold the cats while you drive. Remember to drive very slowly since the storm is so bad.

Reader 2   Don't worry. We'll make it to Grandpa's house.

Reader 1   I hope our house makes it through this storm.

Reader 2   At least we will. Off to Grandpa's house!

Developing Reading Fluency • Gr. 3 © 2003 Creative Teaching Press

The Secret Sack

Genre: mystery

Characters: Friend 1 and Friend 2

Friend 1   Are you ready to play a game? You will get five clues. The object of the game is to guess what I am hiding in my secret sack before I tell you all five clues. Here we go.

Friend 2   That sounds so fun. I'm ready. What is my first clue?

Friend 1   You can hold it in your hands.

Friend 2   I'm going to guess that it is a rubber ball.

Friend 1   Not even close, but good try! Here's your next clue. You can eat it, but you don't need to use any silverware.

Friend 2   Wow, that is a great clue! Let me see. I can hold it in my hands and eat it without silverware. Is it an apple?

Friend 1   No, but that was another smart guess. You are trying to think of something that could fit in this bag aren't you? Clever thinking! This next clue should help you a bit more. There are many pieces in this bag.

Friend 2   Oh, so it's not just one item! You have many pieces of something I can hold in my hands and eat without any silverware. Is it candy?

The Secret Sack

Friend 1   No, but that would make sense with the three clues I have given you so far. Here is your fourth clue. It changed form when it was heated.

Friend 2   Oh, my! Let me see. It is a bag full of small items I can eat without silverware and it looks different now than before it was heated. Is it some chocolate-covered peanuts?

Friend 1   No, but that was your closest guess so far. Are you ready for your fifth and final clue? It is a snack that you can pop into your mouth.

Friend 2   Give me a little time to think about this one. This is tricky. Let me get all of my clues straight. It's a food I can eat without silverware that has changed form after being heated and I can pop it into my mouth?

Friend 1   I will tell you that one word in the last clue is a big hint!

Friend 2   A snack that you can pop into your mouth?

Friend 1   That's right! What is it?

Friend 2   I know! It's popcorn!

Developing Reading Fluency • Gr. 3 © 2003 Creative Teaching Press

Playground P.I.'s

Genre: mystery

Characters: Friend 1 and Friend 2

Friend 1   Wow! I can't believe our teacher chose us to be the Playground P.I.'s this week.

Friend 2   I'm pretty surprised myself. By the way, what does the P.I. stand for?

Friend 1   That's short for private investigator.

Friend 2   Well, that makes sense to me, since our main job is to help people solve playground problems and mysteries. Do you think we will have any interesting cases this week?

Friend 1   I hope so. Last week, the Playground P.I.'s got to help the custodian solve the Case of the Missing Trash Can Lid.

Friend 2   I'm sure it was a DIRTY job, but someone had to do it!

Friend 1   I only hope we get to keep our hands clean.

Friend 2   Hey, look! I see a girl crying over by that tree. It could be our first case. Let's go over there to see what's going on.

Friend 1   Great idea!

Friend 2   Hello, we're the Playground P.I.'s. Do you have a problem we can help you solve?

Developing Reading Fluency • Gr. 3 © 2003 Creative Teaching Press

Playground P.I.'s

Friend 1   Oh, your jacket is missing and you think your parents are going to get mad at you.

Friend 2   That sounds like a case for us to solve. Are you ready?

Friend 1   Don't cry! We'll help you find your jacket. This is the Case of the Missing Jacket and we're going to crack it by the end of the day.

Friend 2   What's your name?

Friend 1   What room are you in?

Friend 2   Where did you last see your jacket? What does your jacket look like?

Friend 1   We'll find your jacket and send it to your room. For now, try not to worry about it.

Friend 2   Let's check the lost and found baskets first.

Friend 1   Great idea! Then if we don't find it, we'll search the area between the classroom and the playground.

Friend 2   I'll look in this basket for the blue jacket while you look over there.

Friend 1   Hey, here it is! We solved the Case of the Missing Jacket.

Friend 2   That was too easy. I hope the next case we get is a little more challenging.

Developing Reading Fluency • Gr. 3 © 2003 Creative Teaching Press

The Writing Contest

Genre: narrative story

Characters: Friend 1 and Friend 2

Friend 1   Did you hear about the writing contest held by the newspaper?

Friend 2   No, I haven't heard about it. What do you have to do and what's the prize?

Friend 1   Well, it's an essay contest. The topic is the nation. You can write about anything that relates to our nation.

Friend 2   Did the newspaper offer any suggestions?

Friend 1   It said that you could write about how to protect our nation, the environment, or the economy.

Friend 2   What's the prize?

Friend 1   The first prize is $150.00. The second prize is a gift certificate for any store in the mall. The third prize is a pizza party.

Friend 2   Are you going to enter the contest?

Friend 1   You bet! I'm a great writer! I think I could win first prize. Do you want to enter the contest, too?

Friend 2   Sure! I think I'm a good writer as well. I already know what I would want to write about—protecting endangered species.

Developing Reading Fluency • Gr. 3 © 2003 Creative Teaching Press

Plays for Two

The Writing Contest

Friend 1   That's a great idea. I'm going to write about air pollution.

Friend 2   Did the newspaper mention how long the essay should be?

Friend 1   The contest rules say that the essay should be no longer than two pages.

Friend 2   Wow! That's short. I'm going to have a hard time putting everything I want to say about endangered species into only two pages.

Friend 1   I know what you mean. Oh, by the way, the newspaper said it was important to mention why you chose the topic, what it means to our nation, and some ideas on how to solve the problem.

Friend 2   I can do that. When is the deadline?

Friend 1   All entries must be received by the newspaper by next Friday. We'd better get started. Good luck!

Friend 2   Good luck to you, too. Even if we don't win, at least we gave it a try!

Developing Reading Fluency • Gr. 3 © 2003 Creative Teaching Press

The Hole

Genre: cumulative tale

Characters: Reader 1 and Reader 2

Reader 1   This is the hole.

Reader 2   This is the rabbit that ran into the hole.

Reader 1   This is the cat that chased the rabbit

Reader 2   that ran into the hole.

Reader 1   This is the dog that chased the cat

Reader 2   that chased the rabbit that ran into the hole.

Reader 1   This is the boy who chased the dog

Reader 2   that chased the cat that chased the rabbit

Reader 1   that ran into the hole.

Reader 2   This is the sister who chased the boy

Reader 1   who chased the dog that chased the cat

Reader 2   that chased the rabbit that ran into the hole.

The Hole

Reader 1   This is the dad who chased the sister

Reader 2   who chased the boy who chased the dog

Reader 1   that chased the cat that chased the rabbit

Reader 2   that ran into the hole.

Reader 1   Why was everyone running in the first place?

Reader 2   It all started when the rabbit ran by the cat.

Reader 1   The cat just had to chase the rabbit! Luckily, the rabbit had a safe hiding place.

Reader 2   What happened when the cat got to the hole?

Reader 1   The dad bumped into the sister who bumped into the boy who bumped into the dog who tripped over the cat that fell into the hole that was made by the clever rabbit!

Developing Reading Fluency • Gr. 3 © 2003 Creative Teaching Press

Getting Wild!

Genre: news report

Characters: Reporter 1 and Reporter 2

Reporter 1 Hello all of you in TV land! Do we have big news for you! Get your pencils ready. We have a phone number you'll surely want to write down.

Reporter 2 That's right, kids! There's a new game show on the XYZ television network. The only contestants will be kids between the ages of 7 and 12.

Reporter 1 They are looking for contestants who like to laugh and have fun!

Reporter 2 Don't forget the most important part—you have to love animals!

Reporter 1 This new game show is a bit like the popular game show *Jeopardy* with a few fun twists for kids.

Reporter 2 Let's tell them how it's similar first.

Reporter 1 Good idea! There are five categories with hidden questions. Every question is worth points.

Reporter 2 It's different because every 60 seconds a gong rings. The contestant with the most points closes his or her eyes and picks an animal card from a treasure chest.

Reporter 1 The animal cards show different wild animals.

Reporter 2 The vet will bring out the wild animal that was on the card for that contestant to pet. The contestant then has a chance to earn some money.

Plays for Two

Getting Wild!

Reporter 1   The contestant has to name three facts about the wild animal. The audience will use electronic keypads to vote on whether or not each fact was important.

Reporter 2   If the audience likes a fact, the contestant earns $25.00.

Reporter 1   As you can see, it's a great way to earn money while having fun with wild animals. Every minute, one contestant has a chance to earn up to $75.00!

Reporter 2   Wow, that could really add up!

Reporter 1   The best part is that you get to be up close with some wild animals you could otherwise only see in a zoo or read about in books.

Reporter 2   So right now you are probably wondering how to sign up. Right?

Reporter 1   Well, we are here to help you out. First, make sure that you are between the ages of 7 and 12 and you have your parents' permission.

Reporter 2   If you like animals, want an adventure, and would like to earn some money to pay for college, then call the XYZ studios at 555-WILD.

Reporter 1   Go tell your parents all about it. Every game show has four contestants. There will be one show a week for twelve weeks.

Reporter 2   If you are ready to GET WILD, then ask your parents if you can call 555-WILD today!

Developing Reading Fluency • Gr. 3 © 2003 Creative Teaching Press

A Room-Cleaning Machine

Genre: invention poem

Characters: Reader 1 and Reader 2

Reader 1   Mom says I need to make my bed.

Reader 2   And after that my dog needs to be fed.

Reader 1   She says my toys need to be put away.

Reader 2   But I play with them every single day!

Reader 1   Why does she want my room to look neat?

Reader 2   She looked in my closet and saw that I cheat.

Reader 1   It doesn't bother me if everything's in a pile.

Reader 2   It sure bothers her. When she is in my room, she won't even smile.

Reader 1   My mom doesn't seem to understand!

Reader 2   My room should look like a kid's land!

Plays for Two

A Room-Cleaning Machine

Reader 1 I admit it is not perfectly clean.

Reader 2 That's why I need a Room-Cleaning Machine!

Reader 1 If only someone would invent one for me.

Reader 2 Millions would be sold—I guarantee!

Reader 1 Every kid's room I've seen is a big mess.

Reader 2 How others clean up, I could only guess.

Reader 1 A Room-Cleaning Machine would save my life.

Reader 2 It would be as popular as a kitchen knife.

Reader 1 It would have to be cheap and easy to store.

Reader 2 I just don't want to clean my room anymore!

Reader 1 Someone, please help me! I'm sure you agree!

Reader 2 A Room-Cleaning Machine—that's the key!

Developing Reading Fluency • Gr. 3 © 2003 Creative Teaching Press

A New World Record

Genre: news report

Characters: Reporter 1 and Reporter 2

Reporter 1   Hello all of you in TV land! We have big news for you!

Reporter 2   Three students from _____ School will be trying to set a new world record tomorrow.

Reporter 1   Yes, and we will be reporting live from _____ School so you can watch the whole event!

Reporter 2   Wait a minute. We haven't told our viewers which record they are trying to break.

Reporter 1   You're right! Well, it may seem a little crazy to you, but these three students are very serious.

Reporter 2   Together they are going to try to send over the Internet the most electronic e-mail cards that have ever been sent in a period of only four hours.

Reporter 1   Yes, that's right! They have VERY long lists of addresses. Their goal is to make it into the world record books in this new area.

Reporter 2   They are willing to let all of our viewers in on the event as well.

Developing Reading Fluency • Gr. 3 © 2003 Creative Teaching Press

A New World Record

Reporter 1   I almost forgot to mention that. If any viewers out there would like to receive an e-mail card as part of this event, the students would be happy to add you to their lists.

Reporter 2   All you have to do is call us at 555-NEWS and give us your e-mail address. We will give it to them when we arrive at _____ School tomorrow.

Reporter 1   Right now, we are conducting a survey on our Web site. You can log onto our Web page and cast your vote about whether or not they will be able to set this new world record.

Reporter 2   What do you think? Will they be able to set this unique Internet record?

Reporter 1   You know what? I think they will be able to do it because they came up with a clever plan and they are very organized.

Reporter 2   How many e-cards do you think they will be able to send in the four-hour time limit?

Reporter 1   Assuming they have their lists well prepared, I predict that they will send 160 e-mail cards.

Reporter 2   What do you viewers out there predict?

Reporter 1   You'll have to tune in to channel 9 tomorrow to see the results!

Reporter 2   We all wish them the best of luck!

Developing Reading Fluency • Gr. 3 © 2003 Creative Teaching Press

The Space Adventure

Genre: space poem (can be read as a limerick)

Characters: Reader 1 and Reader 2

Reader 1   I want to go someplace new.

Reader 2   Forget the aquarium and the zoo.

Reader 1   I want to go someplace way out in space

Reader 2   to see planets and stars. What a view!

Reader 1   My favorite planet of the nine is Mars.

Reader 2   I can't travel there in a car.

Reader 1   Ready or not, someday I'll be an astronaut

Reader 2   and ride in a space shuttle up near the stars.

Reader 1   Our solar system is called the Milky Way.

Reader 2   I plan to investigate it someday.

The Space Adventure

Reader 1   I'll study Saturn and Neptune, the Sun and the Moon.

Reader 2   I'll learn about a galaxy far, far away!

Reader 1   Would you like to go on the adventure, too?

Reader 2   Would you like to discover something new?

Reader 1   Find some other place, way out there in space,

Reader 2   far beyond the sky we see that's blue.

Reader 1   Right now, I'm just a kid with a big dream.

Reader 2   That's how it may look and seem.

Reader 1   But dreams do come true, for me and for you.

Reader 2   One day in the future, I'll be on an astronaut team!

Readers 1 and 2
            You'll see!

Developing Reading Fluency • Gr. 3 © 2003 Creative Teaching Press

The Dollar

Genre: *cumulative tale with a twist*

Characters: Reader 1 and Reader 2

Reader 1	This is the game that we bought.
Reader 2	That is the store where we paid for the game that we bought.
Reader 1	That is the girl who gave us one dollar in change
Reader 2	at the store where we paid for the game that we bought.
Reader 1	That is the customer who bought a puzzle with that dollar that we got in change
Reader 2	from the girl at the store where we paid for this game.
Reader 1	That is the bank where the customer got the dollar
Reader 2	to pay for his puzzle that we later got in change from the girl at the store
Reader 1	when we paid for the game that we bought.

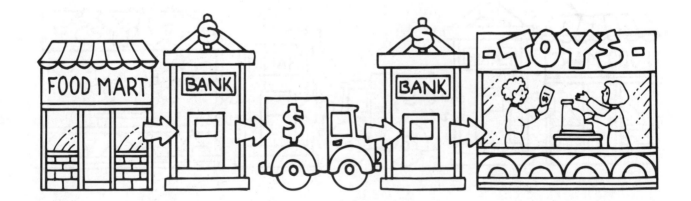

Developing Reading Fluency • Gr. 3 © 2003 Creative Teaching Press

Plays for Two

The Dollar

Reader 2   That is the truck that brought the dollar to the bank

Reader 1   where the man got his money to pay for the puzzle

Reader 2   that he bought from that girl who worked at that store

Reader 1   where we bought this game.

Reader 2   How did the truck get the dollar?

Reader 1   Probably from another store far away

Reader 2   where a customer bought an item and paid for it with that dollar.

Reader 1   The store sent their money to the bank. The truck picked it up

Reader 2   and delivered it to the bank where the man got it to buy his puzzle.

Reader 1   That's when we got the dollar in change when we bought a game. This is the game.

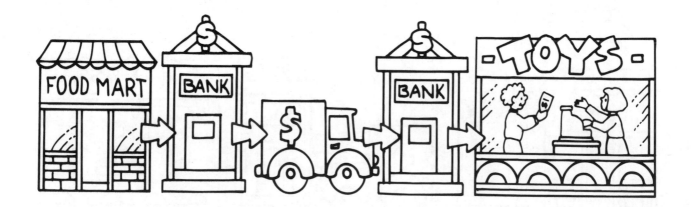

Developing Reading Fluency • Gr. 3 © 2003 Creative Teaching Press

Reader's Theater

Reader's Theater is a motivating and exciting way for students to mature into fluent and expressive readers. Reader's Theater does not use any props, costumes, or materials other than the script, which allows the focus to stay on fluent and expressive reading. The "actors" must tell the story by using only their voices and must rely on their tone of voice, expression, phrasing, and fluency to express the story to the audience. Students are reading for a purpose, which highly motivates them because they take on the roles of characters and bring the characters to life through voice inflection. Each Reader's Theater script is designed for a group of four students. However, the scripts can be modified, if necessary. For example, students can double-up on roles to incorporate paired reading.

Strategies: repeated oral reading model for groups of four, choral reading, paired reading

Materials
- highlighters
- colored file folders
- sentence strips
- yarn

Directions

1. Make four copies of each play. (Each play is several pages long.) Staple together the pages along the left side of the script (not the top). Highlight a different character's part in each script.

2. Gather four folders of the same color for each play. Put one copy of the script in each folder. Write the title of the play and the name of the highlighted character (e.g., The Alien, Linda) on the front of each folder.

3. Divide the class into groups of four. Give each student in a group the same color folder (containing the same script).

4. Have students first read the entire script. (Research supports having students read all of the roles for the first day or two to fully comprehend the story.) Then, have students choose which part they will perform, or assign each student a part. Have students switch folders so that each student has the script with the highlighted character's part that he or she will play.

5. Write each character's name on a sentence strip to make name tags. Hole-punch the name tags, and tie yarn through the holes. Give each student a name tag to wear. Have students spend at least four to five days reading and rereading their part to practice phrasing and fluency.

6. Invite students to perform their play for the whole class, another group, a buddy class, or their parents.

Extension

Invite more advanced readers to choose a script and put on a puppet show with a group. (This type of performance is dramatic play, not Reader's Theater, because students use props with their voices to tell the story.) Invite the group to practice their lines, make puppets (out of paper bags, toilet paper rolls, or craft sticks), and perform the play.

The Alien

Theme: science fiction

Characters: Narrator   Arthur
              Linda   Alien

Narrator
Last night, a mysterious thing happened at the home of Linda and Arthur. Right now they are on the bus going to school. They didn't notice anything different until Linda saw something strange.

Linda
What is that bright light in your backpack, Arthur?

Arthur
What in the world are you talking about? There's no light in my backpack. The only things I have in there are my jacket, homework folder, and library books.

Linda
I see a light shining through your backpack. Open it up! I want to look inside!

Arthur
Fine. See? No light.

Alien
YEEK-LOP-ANNO!

Arthur
Help! Close it quick! What kind of trick are you trying to play on me?

The Alien

Linda
You're the one who's trying to play a trick on me! Open your bag again so I can see how you did that!

Arthur
I'm telling you the truth! I am not trying to play a trick on you at all! I have no idea what just made that noise!

Linda
Well, I think I believe you. Open up the bag so we can take a peek inside. There is something very strange going on inside of that backpack!

Arthur
You're right, but I didn't have anything to do with it. I promise!

Linda
Okay! Okay! I believe you, but we have to get down to the bottom of this. It's very strange! On the count of three we'll open the bag together.

Arthur
Deal! One . . . two . . . three!

Alien
YEEK-LOP-ANNO!

Narrator
They couldn't believe their eyes. It was something truly out-of-this-world. They thought it looked a little bit human but much more like a tiny animal. It was about the size of a child's hand!

Developing Reading Fluency • Gr. 3 © 2003 Creative Teaching Press

The Alien

Linda

I'll handle this. Who are you and where do you come from? By the way, please speak in English if you can.

Alien

YEEK-LOP-ANNO! That means, "Help, I'm scared."

Arthur

Who are you and where are you from?

Alien

I'm NOPPI. I came here with my family on our invisible spacecraft. We arrived on your roof last night. I miss my family!

Narrator

Then the mysterious visitor began to cry.

Linda

Are you from another planet?

Arthur

Don't be ridiculous! Of course it's not. There is no such thing as an alien!

Alien

I am from the planet Shomohs. We are a family in training. We come to your house once a week to see how you all get along. Then we try to love and take care of our planet and each other just like you do.

Arthur

I don't believe a word you are saying! Who talked you into playing this trick on us?

Developing Reading Fluency • Gr. 3 © 2003 Creative Teaching Press

The Alien

Narrator

In between crying sobs, NOPPI explained what happened to him the night before.

Alien

I don't care if you believe me or not. I just want to get back to my family. We were all in your room last night when I jumped inside of this bag. All of a sudden, I was stuck inside! I didn't know how to get out! My family ran to hide in our spacecraft, but I was stuck in here until just now!

Arthur

How did you get stuck in my backpack in the first place?

Alien

One minute I was peeking at your library book about space, and the next minute your mom picked up the bag and closed it. I've been stuck in here since last night! Oh, where is my family?

Linda

We have no idea, but right now we're on a bus ride to school. We won't be able to do anything until we get home from school. You're going to have to go to school with us today.

Alien

Will you help me find my family after school?

Arthur

I promise.

Linda

Me, too!

Developing Reading Fluency • Gr. 3 © 2003 Creative Teaching Press

Reader's Theater

The Alien

Arthur

Here's the plan. You will hide in my backpack all day. I'll carry you around with me, so you won't be scared without anyone you know. After school, we'll take our bus ride home and help you find your family.

Linda

Do you think they are still on the roof?

Alien

They would never leave without me, so I know they are up there worried. I just want to go home.

Narrator

That was the most unusual day for Linda and Arthur at school. Arthur kept his backpack by his desk all day. At recess, he brought it out to the playground. At lunch, he brought it to the tables. Everyone was wondering why, but nobody said a word.

Linda

Finally, we're back on the bus! What a long day! I was so worried that our visitor would get caught. What do you think your teacher would have done if she had found our visitor?

Arthur

I'm so glad we don't even have to think about that!

Alien

Are we there yet?

Narrator

Finally, they arrived safely home. The search for the family began. What do you think happened next?

Developing Reading Fluency • Gr. 3 © 2003 Creative Teaching Press

Jack, Jessie, and the Beanstalk

Characters: Narrator   Jessie
                 Jack   Giant

Narrator
Now, you all know the story of Jack and the Beanstalk. In fact, you have probably heard many different versions of the tale. Some are closer to the truth than others. I'm here to help clear up what really happened after Jack planted the beanstalk.

Jack
I can't believe that greedy giant. He wants to keep everything for himself! He needs to give me that goose that lays the golden egg. It's not his!

Narrator
Jack called his friend Jessie on the phone to provide some backup support. Jack knew how strong and mean the giant could be.

Jack
Do you want to help me, Jessie?

Jessie
Sure. I'll be over in a few minutes. I just have to put on my hiking boots first. It's a long climb up that beanstalk!

Narrator
Jessie put on her hiking boots and then walked over to Jack's house.

Jack, Jessie, and the Beanstalk

Jack

Let's hurry! It's getting dark! My dad will be so happy to have his favorite goose back. We need the money we can get for selling the golden eggs. We don't even have enough money right now for breakfast!

Jessie

I know what you mean. My mom just lost her job, so times are tough at my house, too!

Narrator

They climbed up to the top of the beanstalk. Then, they knocked on the giant's door. Now, you may be wondering why they didn't just sneak in and take the goose back. Well, they are honest citizens. They know it is not legal to enter someone else's house unless that person lets you in. Well, let's get back to the story . . .

Giant

Fee-fi-fiddle-dee-doo. Jack, that better not be you!
Fee-fi-fiddle-dee-dee.

Jack

Yes, it's me. I brought my friend Jessie with me this time. We have a deal for you that you won't be able to pass up.

Giant

Oh, a deal? Let me guess! I give you that silly old goose you keep asking for and you'll let me eat Jessie. Is that the deal?

Developing Reading Fluency • Gr. 3 © 2003 Creative Teaching Press

Jack, Jessie, and the Beanstalk

Jack
Of course not! You have to be serious and at least listen to our deal.

Giant
Oh, come on! I'm a giant. Giants are always scary! I can't change now! I don't have to listen to your deal. I can eat you both!

Jessie
Hello, Mr. Giant! Now, I'll let you know that I just got over the flu. So if you eat me you could catch the flu yourself. I'm sure you don't want that to happen. Right?

Giant
No way! I'm a big, strong giant! I can't get the flu. Okay, you're safe, but I can still eat Jack here.

Jessie
You are so silly! You know you don't want to eat us. You just want to scare us. Now, just relax and listen to our idea.

Jack
We know that you just pick on us because you want the attention. That means that deep down inside you are just lonely. You want someone or something to keep you company. Is that why you have the goose in the first place?

Narrator
Just then the big, strong giant began to cry. Actually, he began to sob!

Developing Reading Fluency • Gr. 3 © 2003 Creative Teaching Press

Jack, Jessie, and the Beanstalk

Giant

Well, I have to admit, it is pretty boring living up here in this great big house all by myself.

Narrator

The giant looked at Jack and then Jessie.

Jessie

We understand. You just want a friend. Well, you are about to get two for the price of one.

Jack

Well, to be honest with you it will be two for the price of one . . . goose!

Giant

Do you mean to tell me that you will be my friend if I give you back your goose?

Jessie

That's right. We'll both be your friends. We'll come up here and have lunch or dinner with you as often as we can.

Narrator

Just then, a huge smile came across the giant's face. The giant, who everyone thought had a heart that was two sizes too small, was so happy!

Developing Reading Fluency • Gr. 3 © 2003 Creative Teaching Press

Jack, Jessie, and the Beanstalk

Giant

I've never had a friend before. I see all of you kids down there laughing and playing with your friends. I've never been able to have a friend.

Jack

It took us a long time to figure that out, but we did. We will be your friends. We will play with you and eat with you.

Giant

Will you play a game with me? I can't play games by myself!

Jessie

Sure we will! Now, are you willing to give Jack his goose back? You know, his family is very poor. They need that goose so they can sell the eggs for money. They need the money to buy food and pay their bills.

Giant

I can do more than that! I'll give you some food, money, and clothes. I will help you since you are helping me. Here, you can have your goose back.

Jack

You won't regret it! We promise to come back whenever you want.

Jessie

How will we know when you want us to climb back up?

Developing Reading Fluency • Gr. 3 © 2003 Creative Teaching Press

Jack, Jessie, and the Beanstalk

Giant

I know! I can stomp my feet. It will make a loud sound like thunder. When you hear that sound, then you will know it's me, your giant friend, asking you to come up and play.

Jack

That's a great idea!

Narrator

They all shook hands to make the deal look official. Secretly, they all planned to keep their word, so the handshakes really didn't matter.

Jessie

We need to get going soon, so our families don't get worried.

Jack

You're right! Time to go!

Giant

Thank you so much! I'll see you soon. I'll have a yummy treat waiting for you in the oven!

Narrator

With that, they all waved good-bye. Jack and Jessie climbed back down the beanstalk. Jack put the goose in with the other geese and hens. Jessie went home. The giant? What do you think he did next?

Developing Reading Fluency • Gr. 3 © 2003 Creative Teaching Press

The Cooking Show Star

Theme: cooking

Characters: Narrator   Mom
                 Chef Combo   Marcus

Narrator
One Saturday morning, Marcus's mom was watching television. There was a commercial for the Handy Dandy Kitchen Master. It was being advertised by Chef Combo.

Chef Combo
Can you believe your eyes? This Handy Dandy Kitchen Master will chop, slice, mix, and dice! You can make salsa, guacamole, or pasta sauce in less than a minute! How can you live without this handy kitchen helper?

Mom
I can't! I have to have one!

Narrator
Marcus's mom decided she just couldn't live without the new gadget, so she went to the phone to order one. While she was on hold . . .

Marcus
Are you sure you really need one of those things? You don't really cook very often. Chef Combo just said that it costs $49.95! That's so much money! What will Dad say?

Narrator
Marcus's mom was just too excited to listen.

Mom
Yes, I'm ready. I'll be paying for it with my credit card. The number is . . .

The Cooking Show Star

Marcus

Wait until Dad finds out about this!

Mom

Are you kidding? I'd love to come on your show! I'd love to be a member of your studio audience! I love food and all of your kitchen helpers. Can my nine-year-old son come along?

Marcus

Oh, no! Please don't make me go! Not a cooking class!

Mom

You're going with me. We're going down to the television studio tomorrow. You'll get to eat terrific food and meet Chef Combo in person!

Marcus

I don't care if I meet Chef Combo. Can't I stay home? Please?

Mom

No, Marcus. You're coming with me. You need to learn a few cooking tips along with me.

Narrator

Marcus was not excited, but he knew better than to argue with his mother. Maybe his dad would get him out of it. Later that night, he was sad to find out that his dad thought it was a great idea for them to go to the cooking class.

Marcus *(sadly)*

What luck!

Developing Reading Fluency • Gr. 3 © 2003 Creative Teaching Press

The Cooking Show Star

Narrator
The next day they drove to the television studio.

Mom
Look, Marcus! There's Chef Combo!

Marcus
Mom, how long is this going to take?

Mom
Look on the bright side. You get to eat dessert before dinner! Come on! Let's go! Smile!

Narrator
They went into the television studio. There were about twenty other people in the audience.

Chef Combo
Welcome! Thank you for coming to our show! As you know, once the television cameras begin rolling, we need you to laugh, cheer, and clap as much as possible! You look like you are ready for a fun and tasty meal! Am I right?

Mom *(loudly)*
Yes!

Chef Combo
I need a volunteer from our studio audience who loves chocolate cake. Who would like to come up?

Mom *(raising Marcus's hand and screaming)*
He will! He will!

Developing Reading Fluency • Gr. 3 © 2003 Creative Teaching Press

Reader's Theater

The Cooking Show Star

Marcus
Oh, please don't do this to me!

Chef Combo (*to Marcus*)
Do you like chocolate cake?

Marcus
Yes, but I don't know how to cook.

Chef Combo
Perfect! I'll show you how easy it is with our new Handy Dandy Magic Mixer! Come on up on stage! You're going to be on TV my friend!

Marcus
Really? Okay.

Narrator
While Chef Combo explained to Marcus what he would be doing, his mother was sitting in the audience with a huge smile on her face. The cameras started rolling.

Chef Combo
Welcome to our show! Today's guest is Marcus. He admits that he doesn't really know how to cook or bake. Today he will show you how easy it is to make a chocolate cake with our new Handy Dandy Magic Mixer.

Narrator
The show continued taping. Marcus was the star of the show. By the time he went to school the next day, most of his friends had already heard about the TV show. He was the star of the school. Can you guess how they found out?

Developing Reading Fluency • Gr. 3 © 2003 Creative Teaching Press

The Airplane Ride

Characters: Narrator   Kimberly
                Efren   Flight Attendant

Narrator

It was the holiday season again. Efren and Kimberly were going to fly to El Paso, Texas, to see some people in their family that they had not seen in a long time.

Efren

Kimberly, we have to hurry! Our flight will leave without us if we're late. This airline is almost always on time. Mom said that she would drop us off at the place where we check in our luggage.

Kimberly

I've already put my luggage into the car. I was waiting for you. If you're ready, then let's go get Mom!

Efren

Mom! We're ready to go now!

Narrator

Their mom drove them to the airport and told them how to stay safe one more time.

Kimberly

Okay, Mom. We promise to stay together at all times.

Efren

We promise to stay with the flight attendant.

Kimberly

We're going to be fine. Sure, we're flying alone for the first time, but we have each other and we know the safety rules.

Developing Reading Fluency • Gr. 3 © 2003 Creative Teaching Press

Reader's Theater

The Airplane Ride

Efren
Try not to worry about us, Mom! We'll call you as soon as we get in and meet Uncle Bob.

Flight Attendant
You must be Efren and Kimberly. Are you ready to fly to Texas? It will be a short flight today with clear skies.

Kimberly
We're all set!

Flight Attendant
Follow me and I'll take you to your seats. You get to sit in the front of the plane. You will get a sandwich shortly after we take off. You also have your own television sets, so you can watch whatever you want on our way to Texas.

Efren
Wow! I didn't know that we would get to watch TV!

Flight Attendant
On our airline, every seat has a TV, so you should enjoy yourselves. I have to go prepare our safety plans right now, but if you need anything, just push this button.

Efren and Kimberly
Thanks!

Narrator
They looked at magazines while they waited for all of the other people to get seated.

Developing Reading Fluency • Gr. 3 © 2003 Creative Teaching Press

The Airplane Ride

Flight Attendant
We are getting ready to take off. Are you okay? Is there anything I can get for you?

Efren
I think we are fine for now. Thank you for checking on us.

Narrator
The airplane doors were shut and the pilot started up the engine. The plane began to back up. They could see that they were about to go down the runway to prepare for the takeoff.

Kimberly
I'm scared. Will we be okay?

Efren
Sure! Do you know how many flights take off and land across the world every single day? We are going to be just fine. Here, you can help me with this word search puzzle I brought.

Kimberly
Oh, good. That will take my mind off of the flight.

Flight Attendant
We're about to take off. Are you two okay?

Kimberly
We're fine, thanks! When will the TV start to work?

Flight Attendant
As soon as we get up into the air you should be able to pick a show. For now, at least you have some fun puzzles to keep you busy. Let me know if you need me.

Developing Reading Fluency • Gr. 3 © 2003 Creative Teaching Press

Reader's Theater

Efren

Thank you!

Narrator

The plane took off smoothly. Before she knew it, Kimberly could watch TV. Efren watched a different show on his TV. There wasn't a single bump on the whole airplane ride! What a great flight!

Kimberly

When we get off, I want to thank the pilot for flying this plane so well!

Efren

That would be a nice thing to do!

Flight Attendant

We are getting ready to land, so make sure you have your seat belts on. Thanks!

Narrator

The plane landed safely. As they walked off the plane, Kimberly said "Great flying" to the pilot. The pilot said, "Thank you so much! Come back and fly with us soon."

Kimberly

Bye. We'll see you next week when we fly back to New York.

Developing Reading Fluency • Gr. 3 © 2003 Creative Teaching Press

The Classroom Competition

Characters: Mr. Arias   Kai
                      Narrator Brenton

Mr. Arias

Good morning, class! Are you ready for another fun day at school?

Narrator

All of the students in the class smile and say "yes." They love Mr. Arias! He is a fun teacher who is always full of surprises.

Mr. Arias

As you know, we've been learning about ways to help our world. Our focus has been on creating less trash, recycling, and using things again and again. Our principal, Mrs. Kominsky, told me that the Classroom Competition begins tomorrow.

Kai

What is the Classroom Competition?

Brenton

Is that what Mrs. Kominsky was talking about at the assembly?

Mr. Arias

That's right! Every classroom will be in charge of collecting cans for recycling.

Kai

Is there a prize for the class that collects the most cans?

Mr. Arias

Yes, there is a prize. However, we will not be collecting the cans just to win the prize. If we win the prize, that will just be an extra bonus. Our focus will be on collecting cans to help our environment.

The Classroom Competition

Narrator
At this point, some students started to talk about what kinds of soda they drink at home.

Mr. Arias
Okay, it doesn't matter what kind of soda it is. All that matters, is that we collect the cans to recycle.

Brenton
We already recycle at my house. We have two trash cans. We put the cans in one and the trash in the other.

Mr. Arias
Terrific! Do you think you could bring the cans to school instead? They will still get recycled.

Brenton
I'll ask my dad. I'm sure it will be fine with him.

Kai
My family doesn't drink soda. What can I do?

Mr. Arias
You can be in charge of crushing the cans when they come to class.

Narrator
Suddenly, the class gets noisy as all of the students want to be the "can crushers." Mr. Arias asks the class to quiet down. It takes only a few seconds and the class is quiet again.

Mr. Arias
That's better. I get the feeling that you all want to help in the can-crushing process. Who has an idea for Kai? How can Kai help us collect cans if her family doesn't drink soda?

Developing Reading Fluency • Gr. 3 © 2003 Creative Teaching Press

The Classroom Competition

Brenton
Maybe she could ask the people she knows who live on her street. Maybe they will bring their cans over to her house.

Mr. Arias
That's one great idea. Does anyone else have other ideas for Kai?

Narrator
The class offers a few more ideas. One idea was for Kai to ask the pizza parlor next to the school to save their cans for the classroom contest. Another idea was for Kai to ask the deli near her house to save its cans.

Kai
I will try. I'll ask my mom to take me to the deli and the pizza parlor.

Mr. Arias
That's all that matters. As long as you try, then you are helping our class. I won't be counting how many cans each of you brings in. We are a team. Our goal is to recycle as many as we can. If we win the Classroom Competition, great. If not, at least we helped the enviroment.

Kai
What is the prize anyway? You never told us.

Mr. Arias
The prize for the class that recycles the most cans is a pizza party.

Narrator
The class gets a bit out of control all over again. They just can't help it! Everyone loves a pizza party!

Developing Reading Fluency • Gr. 3 © 2003 Creative Teaching Press

The Classroom Competition

Brenton
Why can't every class have a pizza party for trying their best?

Mr. Arias
It would cost too much money. Let's not focus on the party anyway. We need to get organized. Where should we put the cans when they arrive?

Kai
We have an extra trash can. It's huge! I could bring it in and we could put all of the crushed cans inside.

Brenton
Then our classroom would smell like a dump!

Mr. Arias
Well, I'm sure that Kai's trash can is clean, so it would not make our classroom smell badly at all.

Kai
I will clean it out and spray it with air freshener before I bring it in.

Narrator
The class starts laughing.

Mr. Arias
That's a great idea! Look how much you have helped us already!

Brenton
When does the contest begin? Should I start saving cans right away?

Developing Reading Fluency • Gr. 3 © 2003 Creative Teaching Press

The Classroom Competition

Mr. Arias
Start saving your cans today. You can begin bringing them into our classroom as soon as Kai's trash can arrives. When do you think you could bring it in?

Kai
I'm sure I could wash and spray it this weekend. That means that I could bring it in on Monday.

Mr. Arias
That will be just fine. Everyone should start collecting cans today. Remember to wash them out before you bring them to class so they don't attract bugs to our room. You can begin bringing them in on Monday.

Brenton
How will we know how many we bring in?

Mr. Arias
That's a good question. I'll give you all two minutes to talk to a partner and come up with a good answer to that question.

Narrator
The class begins whispering ideas to each other. Some children want to make a table with each child's name, some want a bar graph, and others want a tally chart. Mr. Arias lists the choices and asks the class to vote. Then he announces the decision.

Mr. Arias
When you bring in a can, you will place a tally mark on this board.

Brenton
That's the best idea, since we will have hundreds of cans!

Mr. Arias
Great attitude! Start collecting those cans! Now . . . on to math!

Developing Reading Fluency • Gr. 3 © 2003 Creative Teaching Press

Reader's Theater

Phrasing Memory Challenges

Students who are still not reading with phrasing and fluency will have a difficult time with the transition from learning to read to reading to learn, since their comprehension will be significantly impaired. Students who lack phrasing and fluency will be "word reading" rather than reading for meaning. These students need many opportunities to listen to phrasing, practice reading phrased chunks of three to four words, and transfer this practice into ongoing text. The fun, motivating memory challenges in this section provide modeling and practice, while challenging students' auditory memory for phrased units. This puts the emphasis on meaning rather than decoding. As the challenge to add a new word or phrase continues, the sentence becomes longer. The phrases themselves change along the way as well, which helps students understand that phrased chunks hold meaning. Each challenge was designed to be used one-on-one between a teacher and a student or as a peer coaching tool between a fluent reader and a less-fluent reader. By reading in phrases and then building on the phrases, the student practices fluency. The application of these strategies to nonfiction text is key, since many students can read fluently in fiction but sound choppy when reading nonfiction.

Strategies: modeled reading, echo reading, repeated oral reading, meaningful chunks, transfer to nonfiction

Materials
• no additional materials are required

Directions

1. Choose a memory challenge, and make one copy of the reproducible.
2. Sit facing the student. (NOTE: You could also have a peer tutor work with the student.)
3. Begin by reading the first sentence. Tell the student to echo (repeat) the first line using his or her auditory memory of the phrases. (The student does not have a copy of the text.)
4. Then, read the second sentence. (Each line adds an additional word or phrase to the original sentence. In some cases, the sentence is slightly revised to incorporate the new text. This teaches the student that a phrase is a meaningful chunk of words rather than a set number of words read together.) Tell the student to echo the sentence.
5. Continue to model reading the remaining sentences on the reproducible, and invite the student to echo each line.
6. Switch roles with the student, and invite him or her to take the role of the teacher and read the first sentence. Repeat the process of modeling and echoing as described in steps 3–5.
7. Then, ask the student to read the nonfiction paragraph at the bottom of the reproducible. This text begins with the complete sentence the student just practiced. This part of the activity provides the transfer process to reading nonfiction text fluently.

Extension

Incorporate choral reading (teacher and student reading together) into this activity for students who have difficulty reading the nonfiction paragraph at the bottom of the page.

My School

I see a school.

I see   a big school.

I see   a big red school.

I see   a big red school   with a yard.

I see   a big red school   with a yard   full of children.

I see   a big red school   with a yard   full of children
who like to play.

I see   a big red school   with a yard   full of children
who like to play soccer   on the field.

I see a big red school with a yard full of children who like to play soccer on the field. At recess time, you can see these children setting up for the soccer game on the field. Do you like to play soccer? Soccer is possibly the most popular sport in the world. Two teams of eleven players try to guide a ball into goal cages at opposite ends of a playing field.

Phrasing Memory Challenges

The Lizard

This is a lizard.

This is a pet lizard.

This pet lizard is a reptile.

This pet lizard is a cold-blooded reptile.

This pet lizard is a cold-blooded reptile that likes to eat crickets.

This pet lizard is a cold-blooded reptile that likes to eat live crickets.

This pet lizard is a cold-blooded reptile that likes to eat live crickets every day.

This pet lizard is a cold-blooded reptile that likes to eat live crickets every day. Do you know what a reptile is? Reptiles are vertebrates, which means that they have a backbone. They breathe air with lungs like you and me. Their skin is covered with scales or plates. All reptiles are cold-blooded like this pet lizard, which means that they depend on their environment for body heat. There are almost 6,000 species of reptiles in the world. Perhaps you will have one as a pet someday!

Future Goals

Do you know   what you want?

Do you know   what you want to be?

Do you know   what you want to be   when you grow up?

Do you know   what you want to be   or do for a living

      when you grow up?

Do you know   what you want to be   or do for a living

      when you grow up   and have to get a job?

Do you know what you want to be or do for a living when you grow up and have to get a job? If you don't, there is no reason to worry yet. According to the United States Department of Education, you should learn about the world around you. As you learn, you will discover what you are interested in. That is why learning is so important for you right now. The key to knowing what you want to become is discovering what you enjoy and what interests you. The only way to do that is to study and learn. So keep up the good work!

The Rain Forest

What can you find?

What can you find   in the rain forest?

What can you find   deep in the rain forest?

What can you find   hidden deep   in the rain forest?

What can you find   hidden deep   in the rain forest canopy?

What can you find   hidden deep   in the hot, still air

    of the rain forest canopy?

What endangered animals   can you find   hidden deep

    in the hot, still air   of the rain forest canopy?

What endangered animals can you find hidden deep in the hot, still air of the rain forest canopy? There are many endangered species fighting to survive in the rain forest. Some of them are the mangrove hummingbird and the squirrel monkey. You can also find birds and monkeys looking for food, flowers blooming, or butterflies flying around in the canopy. Would you like to help these animals?

Developing Reading Fluency • Gr. 3 © 2003 Creative Teaching Press

Earthquakes

Have you ever felt   an earthquake?

Have you ever felt   a trembling earthquake?

Have you ever felt   the rocking   of a trembling earthquake?

Have you ever felt   the rocking and rolling   of a trembling earthquake?

Have you ever felt   the rocking and rolling   or heard the sounds

     of a trembling earthquake?

Have you ever felt   the rocking and rolling   or heard the sounds

     of dishes falling   as a result   of a trembling earthquake?

Have you ever felt the rocking and rolling or heard the sounds of dishes falling as a result of a trembling earthquake? Do you know what causes an earthquake? An earthquake is the vibration of the earth's surface after energy is released from the earth's crust. The crust bends and then snaps into a new position. As it snaps and breaks, vibrations move outward along the surface. The vibrations make the earth shake.

Phrasing Memory Challenges

Kennedy Space Center

Have you ever been   to Kennedy Space Center?

Have you ever been   to Kennedy Space Center   in Florida?

Have you ever been   to see a launch   at Kennedy Space Center
     in Florida?

Have you ever been   to see a shuttle launch   at Kennedy Space Center
     in Florida?

Have you ever been   to see a shuttle launch   or take a tour
     at Kennedy Space Center   in Florida?

Have you ever been to see a shuttle launch or take a tour at Kennedy Space Center in Florida? It is located at Cape Canaveral in the sunny state of Florida. There is an astronaut there every day. He or she answers questions and talks about space missions. You can observe space shuttles and launches. You can also watch an IMAX® movie and learn about space exploration. You can even view the actual *Saturn V* moon rocket! In a word, it's a blast!

Intervention Instruction

Every section in this book can be used throughout the year to teach, guide, practice, and reinforce reading with phrasing and fluency, which will improve students' reading comprehension. The following activities provide additional practice and instruction for those students who need more help with the strategies that will help them improve their reading fluency. Assess students' stage of fluency development often by referring to the chart on page 7.

Use the following activities with "robotic readers" to help them be successful. The activities in this section will help students focus on the following strategies: phrased reading, automaticity with high-frequency words, recognition of what fluency sounds like at the listening level, and active listening.

Each activity includes an objective, a materials list, and step-by-step directions. The activities are most suited to individualized instruction or very small groups. The activities can be adapted for use with larger groups or a whole-class setting in some cases.

Strategy: explicit phrasing

Objective: Each student will practice reading phrases of increasing length with fluency.

Materials
• Pyramids reproducible (page 89)

Directions

1. Give each student a Pyramids reproducible.
2. Discuss the sample in the first pyramid. Model how to read each line of increasing length as one continuous phrase. (Option: Use guided practice following the Fantastic Five Format described on page 8.)
3. Brainstorm topics that students can write about to create sentences for the blank pyramids.
4. Have each student write a sentence in the blank pyramid (using the same format as the example).
5. Read aloud each student-written pyramid to further model phrasing to the group.
6. Invite students to switch papers with a classmate and read each other's sentences.
7. Optional: Have students draw pyramids and write additional sentences.
8. Invite students to discuss what they learned by completing this activity.

I
I want
I want to
I want to get
I want to get a
I want to get a big
I want to get a big brown
I want to get a big brown dog.

Pyramids

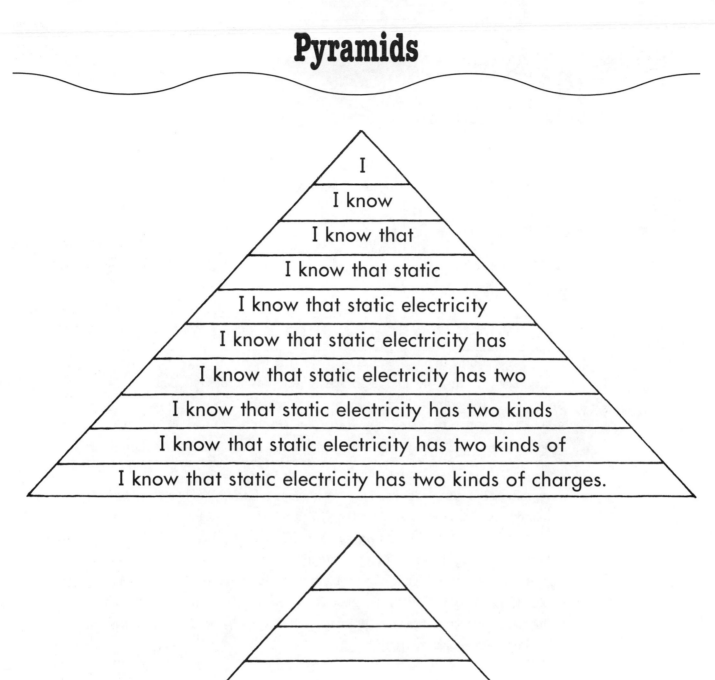

I
I know
I know that
I know that static
I know that static electricity
I know that static electricity has
I know that static electricity has two
I know that static electricity has two kinds
I know that static electricity has two kinds of
I know that static electricity has two kinds of charges.

Intervention Instruction

Strategy: explicit phrasing

Objectives: Each student will understand what phrasing sounds like and looks like in text. Each student will transfer phrasing and fluency to ongoing text.

Materials
- Camping in the Mountains 1 and 2 reproducibles (pages 91–92)
- A Surprise Party 1 and 2 reproducibles (pages 93–94)
- familiar children's books

Directions

1. Copy a class set of the Camping in the Mountains 1 and 2 reproducibles.

2. Divide the class into small groups. Write in each blank the name of a student in the group you are working with.

3. Give each student the Camping in the Mountains 1 reproducible. Read the text following the Fantastic Five Format (described on page 8).

> **Step 1:** Model how to read each phrase.
> **Step 2:** Echo reading—Read one phrase at a time as students repeat.
> **Step 3:** Choral reading—Guide students as they read with phrasing.
> **Step 4:** Independent reading—Have students read the phrases without you.
> **Step 5:** Reverse echo reading—Have students read the phrases, and then repeat them.

4. Give each student the Camping in the Mountains 2 reproducible. (It has the same phrases as reproducible 1, but it is written in an ongoing text format and has an additional paragraph of related text. This reproducible is the KEY! It is very important that you do not skip this reproducible because students will practice transferring their skills of reading phrases fluently to reading sentences in a paragraph fluently.)

5. Choral read the reproducible together. Then, invite the group to read it aloud to you.

6. Repeat the activity with the A Surprise Party reproducibles for further practice.

7. Invite students to practice their phrasing and fluency by reading a familiar book. Easy guided reading books are perfect.

Camping in the Mountains 1

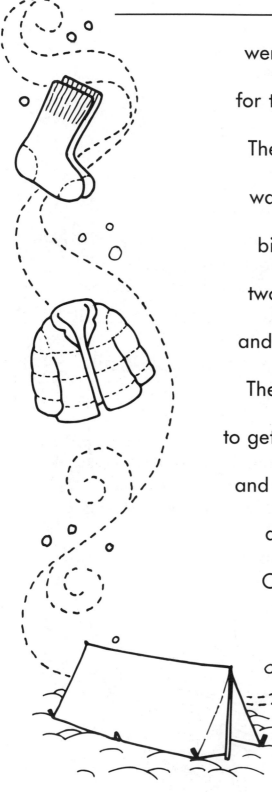

_____ and _____

were busy packing

for the camping trip.

They each packed

warm wool socks,

big snow boots,

two warm jackets,

and a sleeping bag.

They couldn't wait

to get to the mountains

and throw snowballs

at each other.

Off they went!

Camping in the Mountains 2

_____ and _____ were busy

packing for the camping trip. They each packed

warm wool socks, big snow boots, two warm jackets, and a

sleeping bag. They couldn't wait to get to the mountains and

throw snowballs at each other. Off they went!

They got there faster than they ever thought they would.

Along the way, they had been telling jokes, singing songs, and

playing car games. As soon as they arrived, they hopped out

of the car. The first thing they did was unpack, of course.

Then, they ran right out into the snow. They built a fat

snowman, made snow angels, and rolled big snowballs for the

snowball fight! Luckily, they had packed just the right

clothes for the cold weather!

Developing Reading Fluency • Gr. 3 © 2003 Creative Teaching Press

A Surprise Party 1

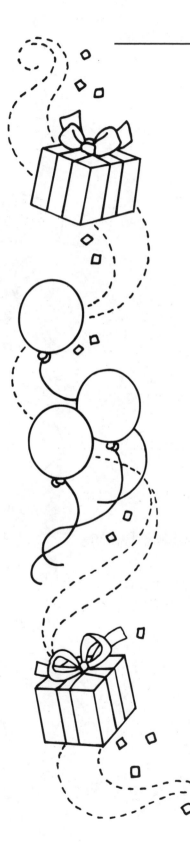
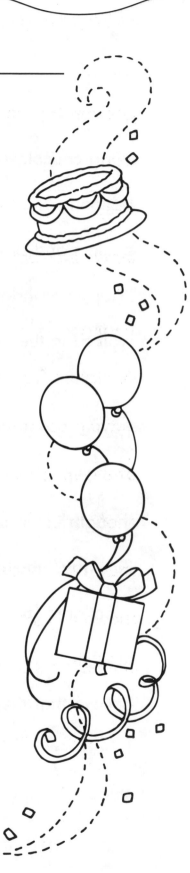

_____ and _____

planned a surprise party

for their teacher.

They brought presents,

a big chocolate cake,

and twenty colorful balloons.

They decorated the room

with posters and signs.

They told the class

to sing "Happy Birthday"

as soon as their teacher

walked in the door.

What a great surprise!

Intervention Instruction

A Surprise Party 2

_____ and _____ planned

a surprise party for their teacher. They brought presents,

a big chocolate cake, and twenty colorful

balloons. They decorated the room with

posters and signs. They told the class to sing

"Happy Birthday" as soon as their teacher

walked in the door. What a great surprise!

That was the last thing their teacher was

expecting! What a terrific surprise from a very

thoughtful class. The students all sang "Happy

Birthday," they shared the cake, and each student took home

a balloon. The students even had a few presents for their

teacher. What an exciting day! They couldn't

believe that they were able to keep their secret!

It had been planned for over a week and not one

student gave away the secret!

Developing Reading Fluency • Gr. 3 © 2003 Creative Teaching Press

Strategy: explicit phrasing

Objectives: Each student will understand why punctuation is so important. Each student will identify punctuation in text that is read aloud and apply this in reading and writing.

Materials
- scissors
- small index cards
- short stories or books

Directions

1. Cut small index cards in half. Give each student four cut cards.
2. Tell students to draw a period, a question mark, an exclamation point, and quotation marks on separate cards.
3. Read aloud a short story. Tell students to hold up a card to indicate the type of punctuation needed in the sentence. For example, as you change speaking voices for different characters, they will hold up the quotation marks. If you ask a question, they will hold up a question mark.
4. Explain to students that good stories have sentences that use different kinds of punctuation. They are not all simple sentences or statements.
5. Invite students to work with a partner. Have the pair take turns reading a short story or book to each other. Tell the listener to hold up the index card that indicates what punctuation he or she hears at the end of each sentence. Then, invite partners to switch roles.
6. Remind students that good readers and writers pay close attention to the punctuation clues. Encourage them to do this when they read and write.

Intervention Instruction

In some severe cases, students have never moved beyond one-to-one matching of every word to speech. This usually causes students to "voice point," which sounds robotic. If a student moved into silent reading before becoming fluent, he or she will "eye point." Fluent readers see at least three to five words ahead of their speech. That's how fluent readers know when to change their voice, form a question, or act surprised. A student who reads one word at a time cannot do this, since his or her eyes only see the word being read. This activity is designed to be used daily for 3 to 5 minutes to transition students from the eye-point and voice-point stage to reading in phrases.

Strategy: explicit phrasing

Objectives: Each student will retrain the way his or her eyes look at print. Each student will learn to look at words in groups rather than in isolation. Each student will move from decoding to comprehending.

Materials
- overhead transparency/projector
- sheet of paper

Directions

1. Use this activity with students who have severe phrasing and fluency problems. Meet with students individually or in small groups for about 3 to 5 minutes daily.
2. In advance, think of a few two-word and three-word phrases (e.g., My house, is blue, It has, a big yard). Write them on an overhead transparency.
3. Cover all of the phrases with a sheet of paper, and leave the overhead projector turned off.
4. Tell the student that you will show him or her one phrase for 1 second. (You will need to be fast. Flip the projector on and off so quickly that the student must visually attend to and recognize all words at once. Do not allow time for reading. Make sure your phrases consist of very easy words.)
5. Move the sheet of paper down so only one phrase is showing on the transparency. Flip the projector on and back off QUICKLY, showing only one phrase.
6. Ask the student to say the phrase.
7. Repeat this process with five to eight phrases each day. Increase the number of phrases as the student's learning improves.